I love love.

poetry & prose
written by

Varsha Iyer

To

the ones that make me feel,
the ones that inspire,
and the ones that remind me why
I love love
so much.

Special Thanks To

Jewel Bell — without you, I would not have
the courage or motivation to write this book.
Thank you for reading my first drafts when you're
too tired, too stressed, too swept up in life.
Thank you for being my biggest fan
and loving me for my truest self
regardless of space, time, and energy.

You show me what strength is every day.
I love you.

Preface

Love comes in many different forms. For me, love is both the good and the bad; it's the pain that succumbs you when you love so much your heart hurts and it's the pleasure that succumbs you when you love so much your heart hurts. It's a double-edged sword. For others, love is only good; it's easy, painless, fluid. Sometimes love is equivalent to affection and other times - affection is minimal but that maximizes the love.

It's funny. I never wanted love to be the central theme of my first book. I didn't want it to define me. But the course of my life and natural progression of my life has shown me time and time again, love is important. Every kind of love is essential to your being in some shape or form: familial love, platonic love, romantic love, love for music, love for the arts, love for nature, love for animals, love for everything and anything that surrounds you.

For some, finding that love is difficult. For others, it comes easy. For me, it's natural. I gravitate towards love. I love reading about love. I love researching historical figures who were so in love it led to mass destruction or they were so in love it let to personal destruction. I love listening to stories about love from my family, my great grandmother, my parents. I love watching my friends fall in love with life, with people, with places. I love feeling everyone else's love so deeply within my heart. I love knowing love is truly subjective; no one can define what it means to you unless it's yourself.

I love love. I love falling in love. I love the stages leading up to it. I love the liking part, the lusting part, the falling part, the loving part. I love the subtle details that you notice, the intimacy, the dramatic but euphoric scenarios you create in your mind, and the feelings it all evokes. But I also have a lot of gratitude for the other side— the side of things that isn't as pretty, isn't as happy, isn't as filled with sunshine.

For some reason, I find so much beauty where beauty seems to be neglected. In heartbreak, you come alive. There are so many visceral emotions, ones that you never thought you inhabited or ones you always avoided and never came to contact with. When you heal, you learn so much about yourself; you are put in a position of discomfort and are forced to grow. And at the root of it all, at the source, there lies love. Pure, simple yet so complicated, absolutely fascinating love.

I love knowing that there is a balance to all my emotions, all my relationships, all my love: both good and bad. I love knowing that the good and the bad push me to grow and become a better person.

I'd like to think I am in love with too much yet not enough. I fall in love with everything I see, everything I do. I fall in love with how deeply I feel. I fall in love how much I care for others. I fall in love with not being in reality and creating daydreams where true euphoria exists. I fall in love with reality and the brashness of making you realize the hard truths of life. I love how the balance in all of this, in love, has led me to write this book.

When I first had the idea for this book, I was having an emotionally tough time trying to learn more about myself and why I constantly love harder than others, why loving others was easier than loving myself, why I fall in love with love so hard and what love is and how love works. I was in this awkward place of being still while the world around me was quickly and constantly changing.

After months of hard work and self-doubt, this book is a culmination of the words that came to me from feelings I felt when I was overwhelmed by the people I've met throughout my life that have impacted my life in some form, somehow through some version of love.

I was inspired every day by different people— the men I have fallen in love with, the men I have been infatuated with, the men who broke my heart, my friends who have loved me and stuck by through the rough times who I would give my heart and soul to at any given moment, the friends who have walked out of my life who I miss every day and leave me wondering about the memories we never made, and more than anything else: myself. I have fallen in love with myself during this period of my life in a way I have never felt before. My growth and journey is due to these emotions that forced me out of my comfort zone— because of love.

And so, with so much sitting in my heart, I did what I do best, I wrote. I spent hours writing poems and prose in order to heal my heart and flesh out my inspiration to its last thread. The collection of writings are in no particular order other than two categories: lovesick & heartache. Each is its own individual being and behind every one, there is a story. This book is something really special to me and something I hope you find just as special too. It's the beginning of my growth in my career as a writer and I thank you for coming along on my journey to see where I'll go from here.

Without further ado, here's "I love love."

—Varsha Iyer

lovesick

you slipped my mind
and my heart caught you
without skipping a beat

as if deep beneath all the
rushed back and forth
of each thought
running; running; running
through my mind,

there lies a small crevice
in which you fit perfectly in.

it's almost as if
you've made it your home
installing a fail-safe,
something so secure
to make yourself known,
to remind me that you're still there,
that you'll always be there.

and so,
you slip my mind
just so i can catch you
before you fall.

— *slipped*

last night,
i dreamt about you
for the first time.

we are laying in bed,
silk sheets messy.

i am just as nervous as
i would have been in real life.

there's something so dreamy
about the natural sun in your apartment.
it makes me less nervous, more calm;

i fall in love with it.

our bodies are so close but not touching.

when we turn to look at one another,
our heads graze by the other's
like honey dripping from a honeydripper—
slowly, softly, but only for a moment
that feels like forever.

we are in a daze.

our arms are extended
in the air towards each other,
elbows bent slightly;

fingers mindlessly touching,
tracing patterns that fill
the silence with their own intimacy
in their own language
that only our bodies understand.

your favorite vinyl is playing
on the record player.

i think about how you told me that
you like to watch it spin.

i want to watch you watch me spin,
i want to be just as mesmerizing,
i want to be your favorite song;

so much so, my voice is the only thing
stuck in your head after i have left you.

i tell you this,
and you smile.

there's something so soft about your smile.

the butterflies in my stomach swoon
at the thought that i am the reason for it.
they flutter faster, and my heartbeat races.

you stop the record player;
i wonder if you can hear my heartbeat.

you watch me spin;
i spin again and again and again.

last night,
i dreamt about you
for the first time
and i didn't want to wake.

—*spinning*

i am dripping in love.

if it were a color of paint, it would be liquid gold.
so bright yet subtle at the same time.
the gold glistens on my skin,
hypnotizing to anyone that comes near.
wherever i move, whatever space i occupy,
i show up dripping in love.

like honey pouring endlessly out of my skin.
like the light reflecting on the ocean from the moon -
its aching love for the waves incessantly
crashing shown by blue light,
illuminating its beauty for the world to see.

i drip, drip in love.
i can't help but drip in love.
it just gets messy so easily.
when you touch me, your hand is thickly coated.

honey is sweet but sticks everywhere.

i drown in it.
my breath catches when i'm pulled under
but it feels so good.
maybe i'm addicted.
there's never enough gleaming gold.
never enough love.

are you overwhelmed?

i am dripping in love.

like the softness of rose petals
dropping against skin, silk against flesh.

i almost feel naked without it.

i could never soften the strength of its intensity
it feels wrong to do anything but engulf myself
with this feeling of warmth, safety.

i want to show up with as much love as i can.
i will never tone it down.

it's all love, it's always love.

liquid gold on my fingertips
honey swirling in my mouth
sickly sweet vanilla coated lips

do you feel it?

i drip, drip with love.
i can't help but drip with love.
i fall in love with it.

—dripping in love

do you remember that night you called me?

we were three months into dating
and you went to a three day music festival
with your best friend who had surprised you
with tickets over breakfast the day before.

do you remember you were slightly drunk?

after the first night finished,
and you called me while the two of you
were walking to his car because
you just missed me so much
you couldn't wait until you got home.

your best friend asked who you were calling
and when you said my name
with a smile in your voice,
i grinned so hard you could hear it.
my aching heart flung out of my chest and into my hands.

in that moment, my name found its home in your voice.

he grabbed the phone from you because he wanted to talk
to the girl he'd been hearing so much about.

"what's your favorite color?" was the only thing he asked.

you took the phone away from him before i could answer,
but i didn't mind because you answered for me
in such a gentle voice that opened up
the palm of my hands to release
my heart to be given to you.

with you, i knew it would be safe.

"black's her favorite even though i keep telling her
it's not even a color and it doesn't count."

i tried to stifle my laughter because when i first told you
black was my favorite color you told me how
as an artist, you wouldn't ever let it slide but—
for me, anything.

your best friend seemed impressed
at how easy you caved in with me.

you seemed impressed
that i trusted you to keep my heart safe.

do you remember that night?

i remember it so clearly;

it's been a year since that night
and it's all i can think about.

how every second you were there
you imagined me with you,
how every second you were there
you were sad watching all of the couples
because you wanted me there with you,
how much you wanted me even though
it had only been three months.

that was the first night
i started falling in love with you.

                    —on a rainy october night in 2017

i speak in love letters.
it's its own language.

each word curved,
like the shape of the tip of your tongue
tracing down soft skin. slow, steady

as if it's memorizing every detail,
and the way i react to your touch.
as if the chills that run down my spine
have no choice but to run as fast as they can.
i hold onto you so tight, you like it that way.

each sentence arched,
like my body bending in the air
from whispers of how i make you feel,
how you make me feel,
with just a touch. i speak

in love letters.

mine are more intense than any other kind.
you'll want to keep them forever.
reading it over and over and over,
until your eyes are glazed
and you can't read anymore.
and the only thing you can do is listen,
in silence, in awe
of what's in front of you:

me.

—keep my love letters safe

if i were an ocean, he would be the moon in control of calming the waves during high tide when all they want to do is crash into each other. there's no other way to write that poetically but i imagine the moon falling in love with the ocean bringing it closer and closer is in itself the most poetic form of beauty. with every move closer, the water gets more passionate trying to reach the moon; it's a dance they each already know the moves to somehow, someway and neither one of them question it. they just move, so natural others marvel at the sight of it.

there's something either really scary or really intimate about feeling too much after 20 days. every 12 hours and 25 minutes, the tides switch from low to high. in 20 days, the ocean would experience high tide 245 times. if i were an ocean, would it only take 245 times to feel the gravitational pull of the moon like an ache pulling on a heart after dipping its edges into something different than what it is used to?

the ocean cannot lie much like the moon cannot deny its beauty. there's something genuine about understanding the truth about it all, the familiarity in both of their actions. if 20 days feels like three months, does it really even matter if it's too scary or too intimate? the high tide will come either way.

"*i love you.*"

the words that leave his mouth resemble the pattern of waves. they curl so tenderly, effortlessly on his tongue and break down into fragments of emotion in my ear. curling inwards, caving inwards to break onto shore. the way his voice stays so steady, so *sure* as they softly breath into my ear is calming; that same tongue that was once a home to his words trailing down my face, my neck, my body as if using it as a canvas. i have never been a piece of art, but if he's holding the tip of the brush then maybe i could be his next masterpiece.

my fingers graze the smoothness of his skin as if they're tracing lines in the sand beckoning the water to come close; my nails at the surface as i watch mesmerized as his eyes roll back in pleasure. the waves are quicker, more intense. i wonder if he can feel in his mind what i am thinking in my mind. do our heartbeats both get faster or is it just mine? if i were an ocean, would my high tide be so strong that the moon must pull back? if the moon was the reason for the high tide, who is at fault— the moon or the ocean?

"*don't dive too deep.*"

it takes 6 hours and 12 and a half minutes for the water at the shore to go from high to low tide and then low to high tide, but it takes him one kiss to balance the pressure. it's easier to swim in my own ocean this way. but the further down i go, the harder it is to hold my breath for that long.

when you dive deep into the ocean, what do you find? what will fill up your ears and your eyes and your mouth before my breath lets up? which is easier— drowning with the knowledge of what's in the deepest part or drowning without the knowledge of what inhabits that world? is it better to leave it untouched or does the beauty of it lie in consuming every inch of it?

the reflection of the moon against the ocean is something extraordinary. the light illuminates the water yet the deeper you dive, the darker it will be. yet the deeper you dive, the warmer it gets. it spreads across enveloping the ocean in its entirety of beauty.

if i were an ocean, he would be the moon in control of how high the high tide should be and how the waves crash so sweetly against his lips tasting like salt waiting anxiously for the end knowing the high tide will end as it always does.

—*don't dive too deep*

by the river,
i left all my clothes. i swam
in slow, letting the water
submerge every inch of me.

my skin felt so soft under the sun,
softer under the waves.
they crashed against each other,
floating me along.

by the river,
my name touched
the lips of a lover.
i'd never heard it
said like that before.

i fell in love with the way it sounded,
with the way it bounced on his tongue
gently, carefully, as if without care,
my name would break into pieces.

i made him say it again and again and again,
until he was out of breath, gasping for air
and the smile on my face started to hurt.

if bliss was a place, this was it.

        —*that day, we wished we could freeze time.*

i wrote a love letter to myself. when i saw
it in the mail, my eyes lit up like
a balloon filled with confetti had popped
above my head. tiny pieces of paper
falling everywhere, tangled in my hair,
sticking to my lips. i smile

so wide; it swallows all the sadness
that had taken refuge in my heart
as i rip apart the envelope
last-week-me had carefully licked
the edges to close it perfectly.

i separate eight pages filled with
words that are heavy, pulling me down
like gravity. i sift in haste, quickly
and the excitement fills my veins
as i blush— blood rushing to my cheeks
and to the tip of my nose
spreading warmth.

my words interrupt my eagerness
forcing me to slow down. i tell myself
i wrote these words for me to really listen,
to sit and really really listen.

they read like poetry—

"make mistakes and bask in
the discomfort that your body writhes in.
change is coming. you will love
the way you drive to work as the sun rises,
purple hues mixed with orange somehow
working when it shouldn't.
stare out the side of the window on the driver's side

but not too long. glimpses of beauty
can sustain you longer than you'd think.
kiss your own skin. your soft lips
will sink into flesh falling onto pillows
loosely fluffed with feathers that fall
when touched. kiss, kiss, kiss.
you are always so afraid of solitude and it saddens
me at how you write about being alone, how you write
about the tears that trail down tirelessly. you
should know that crying every once in a while
relieves the pressure that lives inside of your mind
as it manifests as the ache at the point
where the back of your neck and your shoulder meet.
clean as you go; your mind, your thoughts
are just thoughts in your mind and nothing else.
ask yourself the questions that you never
could answer and take an infinite amount of time to
answer them. there is no deadline
for clarity. in fact, there is no start date.
you can start over at any given moment.
there are no set rules. create your own
and if they refuse to cooperate, train them.
if they refuse to be trained, create new ones.
again and again and again. until you have enough
to wrap your body around and let it hold you up.
change is coming and you need to be
at peace with yourself to welcome it. oh it is so
important to be at peace. you are an
accumulation of all the !'s in every sentence you have
read. intensity is your strongest facet; use it
to your advantage. love yourself with it."

—i wite love letters to myself once a month

living in harmony
in our own little world. i know
you miss it too; you tell me all the time.

domestication is a funny thing when
you're still so young, so naive filled
with "what if"'s and dreams that live in bubbles.

i miss the mundane
filled with words unsaid,
words that can't encompass
how much i love
loading the dishwasher
only ever with you—

soapy dreams, floating above the sink. we
don't have the heart to pop them
as they get higher and higher
until they pop on their own. we hated
seeing them disappear as if they never existed
in the first place. we wanted to be
in love forever as long as forever could stretch
itself to be.

i miss that / "domestication"

when we could pretend bubbles never pop
and hold hands as you press start cycle
on the dishwasher. and i stand on my tip toes
to kiss you for making the mundane
extraordinary.

                    —*our little world was such a dream,*
                    wouldn't you agree?

the blacker the berry,
the sweeter the juice.

i don't know how i always end up
dreaming of you. i associate
fresh fruit with your smile, and i
bite my bottom lip at the thought of a sweet mango,
nectar dripping from your lips.

lemon, ginger, kale, mint—

connections aren't accidents. would you
like to run away with me?

bananas, pineapples, mangos—

leaves sticking to the bottom of our feet
whispering words to each other that
have yet to be said. we run so fast
the whispers get louder and louder
until they catch up to us.

strawberries, blueberries, raspberries—

attraction pulls me in
but depth pulls me deeper. you have
so much of it, so much depth. i want
to eat fresh fruit with you

you and i could be sweet,
covered in blackberries. covered
in each other. let's run away

            —tell me again, what's your
            favorite kind of juice?

heartache

i've always wanted to try vanilla extract
ever since i was young.

just one drop, or maybe one too many
on the tip of my tongue.

but i was always told no —

"*it is so sweet it is bitter.*"

something as simple as a reprimand
intrigues me so much to this day.

how can something be so sweet that it is bitter?

i want to prove those words wrong
with conviction. so badly

so i open the small bottle of unused,
unopened vanilla extract that sits
on the back of the shelf in my kitchen.

i drop one, two, three on my tongue.

my teeth clench but i unclench,
suddenly self-aware
to prove my tastebuds wrong.

my eyes close and i bite my cheek in haste.

i bite so hard that the blood drawn
masks the bitterness.

my conviction doesn't waver
though my experiment failed.

i open my eyes,
i lick my lips,

i smile. the aftertaste is sweet

> — *when you told me, "you're way too sweet"*
> *does that mean you can only take me*
> *in moderation, can only take me one drop*
> *at a time, can only take me mixed with*
> *something? is too much sweetness a bad thing?*

a space cannot be filled
                    where space already exists

you said you needed space
in place of me

within one, two weeks
the silence is deafening

and so i gave you what you want
i thought it would merely exist as a placeholder
                    oh, how wrong i was about you

now you only speak to me in my sleep
but i forget what you say when i wake up
                    or maybe i just don't want to remember
because i know you're not coming back

space:
the gray area in which
questions are put on hold
to find out answers
                    space: it cannot be filled

i have a question for you
and when you find the answer don't tell me
keep it to yourself, keep quiet

and let the resentment wither within you
until it takes up so much space
you'll finally understand
what this poem means

               —what did you do with all the space i gave you
                  before you filled it with someone else?

i bought two disposables.
one for each, just for us
but you threw me away
before mine could even be used.

it stares at me from the top of my dresser
mocking me; or begging me to be used— i'm not sure.
you promised me we'd use up both of them until
the clicks ran out and we couldn't wind them anymore.

but the twenty eight clicks on mine are still there,
and i shove the camera in the back drawer of my dresser
where it won't wonder why it isn't being used
or where you went or why i'm hurting so much.

i don't want to break its heart.
i don't want them to know it's disposable like me—

i wonder how many clicks you've used on yours already
on faces that aren't mine,
on smiles that aren't warm like mine,
on lips that can't kiss like mine.

the first four clicks were of me;
you took them the first night we spent together.
i remember feeling so much for you
and something in my gut told me
you were going to break my heart.

when they get developed, what will you do with them?
will you shove them in the back of your dresser drawer?
will you pretend they never existed?
will you pretend i never existed?

—*click, click, click, click*

the day you left my apartment
for the last time,
you left so abruptly.

you kissed me. once, twice
and then you were out the door

just like that.

it was the perfect kind of sunny outside;
you could almost taste the clear blue in the sky,
and feel the sun on your tongue—
a little sour, but still sweet.

it reminds me of how your lips tasted against mine.

i opened the windows as soon as you left;
i turned the air conditioner off,
opened the balcony door,
letting the breeze lighten my feelings
that felt so heavy sitting in my heart.

i played Frank Sinatra all day,
"Moon River" on repeat.

i sat upside down on the black futon,
legs up in the air crossed,
blood rushing to my head,
intoxicated by the thought of you,

wishing i had more nights with you
to slow dance in the dark
with your voice singing softly in my ear
a sound so safe. i want nothing more
but to be so close— i am one with you.

i watched as my heart flew out
to catch up to you as you walked
on the sidewalk to the train station.

i wondered if you could feel it
rest on your shoulder,
slip beneath the sleeves of your shirt
to sit on your chest,
right next to your own heart.

i wondered if you could feel
another heartbeat,
slower than your usual fast one.

the two beats forming a harmony
that quite never matched at the right time.

a strange emptiness swallowed me whole
as you turned blurry in front of my eyes.

your figure becoming just a shadow
as you turned the corner.

the offbeat of our hearts
leaving my line of sight,
leaving without me.

just like that.

now you're gone
and "Moon River" is somehow always on.

—wherever you're going, i'm going your way

i'm seeing double. which one
of you is real?

my hands reach out to grab at
the outlines of your body
but instead they catch air.

i attempt again,
reaching out to grab at
the outlines of your body
but i'm not fast enough.

instead,

i fall on the pavement,
my hands scraping against
the black tar, hot from the sun,
blood smeared against flesh.

i fall on the pavement
where your shadow had just been
but has now disappeared.

i want to call out your name,
but you wouldn't hear me.

i'm not sure it would matter.

if a tree falls in a forest
and no one is there,
does it still make a sound?

—double of you, one of me

if loving you is a bad habit,
then it's the worst one i have.

after four coffees,
three attempts of sleep,
two missed calls,
one left voicemail,
i can't quit you.

it's three in the morning;
i could drown in thoughts of you.

i want to invade your dreams
and arrive unannounced, uninvited
if that's the only place you'll notice me.

i say your name once, twice, thrice
it sounds funny on my tongue
but i won't ever get tired of saying it.

how many times can i say it
before it turns into an echo?

tell me,
do you fantasize about the future?

do you see anyone but yourself?
do you see me beside you?
can you hear me in the back of your mind?
can you hear me call out to you?

—if Narcissus & Echo existed in 2019,
they would be us.

i remember the day you told me
i was the only thing keeping you alive.

i often wonder where
my nightmares were born
but i realize now that
they were carefully crafted
by your unintentionally manipulative mind.

you never meant to do any harm,
never ever ever ever ever. right?

months later, you told me
i put too much pressure on you
and it broke you in two.

how could someone say
i was the only thing
keeping them alive

and then tell me i'm the reason for their sadness?

your words twisted themselves tight
around my throat making me believe
everything that came out of my mouth
was poison to the world,
that everything that i said
was never of any value.

your words dug their sharp nails
against the flesh on my neck.
drawing blood,
seeping out
any residual feelings
i had for you.

i had a killshot target
above my head.
and you killed and shot
as soon as you had the chance.

i used to call you a coward,
but now i think about
how you ever gained the courage
to hurt me like that.

i am almost impressed
at the accuracy of your unintentional
manipulative hit.

i wonder if sometimes
you think about how
i was the only thing
keeping you alive,

because that was the state of being
you hated the most.

—alive

say my name
the same way you say hers.

you can't, can you?

your tongue touches heaven. like
it's been drenched in
the midnight blue waters of the ocean.
the waves calm you.

say her name. i see
the pleasure it brings you.

i stare at your mouth.
the same one that pressed hard
against mine not seconds earlier.

i touch mine.
the aftertaste is now bitter.
i want to get rid of it.

say my name
the same way you say hers.

you can't, can you?

i know you've been repeating
her name under the covers.
i know you've been whispering
her name in the dark.

i know you know you say it
better than you say mine.

i know you know i know it too.

if i asked you why,
i know i'd already know the answer.

if i asked you why,
would you tell me,
"it's because hers taste better,
it slips off smoother.
it feels better."

would it be the first time
you've told me the truth?

> —*i want you to say my name, but i*
> *think you've only ever said it in vain.*

my last internet search: "another word for dirty"

the list seems endless: contaminated, crummy, dusty,
filthy, greasy, grimy, messy, nasty, sloppy, disarrayed,
foul, lousy, mucky, raunchy, scummy, straggly,

and yet there still isn't a word for how you made me feel.

i'm still searching for the right one.

i feel so dirty, so so dirty
dirty, dirty
but i'm tired of feeling dirty;
it's been festering for far too long.

i wish there was another word for what you made me feel.

—dirty, dirty

when i told him
i loved his love playlist,
he told me: "that one? it makes me sick."

he had listened to it too much.

it exhausted him.
it made him nauseous.

i think about if we would've ever owned a cassette deck.
i wonder what cassettes he would buy,
i wonder which ones i would've.

would we buy the same ones?
would we laugh over it?
would we play it late at night when we can't sleep?
would we fall more in love with it playing?
would he get sick of those songs too?

when i think of the playlist he wanted to delete,
i see the love songs we used to listen to together.
i remember feeling a little sick too.

i think about the cassette deck aga—*click*.

i wonder if he would get so sick and
so frustrated and so angry,
he would pull on the brown little thin plastic
that held the cassette together.

i wonder if he would wrap it around my throat
so he wouldn't have to hear me say
"i love your love playlist."

tightly, baby, *tightly*. until my voice ceases to exist.

i don't think you want to hear me tell you i loved you.

you loved me too, remember?
at least that's what you told me.
you pulled too much, baby,
you pulled on the string too much.

now the same love song is stuck on repeat.

it's the one that was playing in my ears
when you told me: "i hate that playlist."

it was about me, though, wasn't it?
you told me that.
late at night once when we couldn't sleep.
we fell more in love that night.

it's-it's stuck-it's stuck on-it's stuck on repeat.

the playlist is long gone,
but the cassette deck is still playing.
i wonder when it will die.

i'm exhausted.

—cassette deck

you asked me to walk across the bridge
that's in front of us.
i tell you i can only do it if i held your hand.
but you push me forward into the rush of incoming traffic.
because: "you should be able to do this by yourself."
key word: *should*
i close my eyes and keep walking.
walking blindly seems safer.
you tell me to keep my eyes open,
but i can't hear you anymore.
i'm too far.
i remember the last time i drove
on this bridge, i saw five dead deer.
i remember i wondered how many dead
deer i have to see before it's considered bad luck.
i look behind me and i see you watching me.
so close, but so far away.
maybe five dead deer is bad luck.
one less and you would be holding
my hand, walking with me.
two less and we wouldn't have
even been near the bridge.
when i open my eyes again,
i have made it to the other side.
i don't remember how much time has passed.
i only remember dead deer on either side,
the blood pooled by heads and the fur gritted with dirt.
i remember feeling sad.
i wish i could've helped them.
i look back but i cannot see you anymore.
why did i have to go alone?
i feel like roadkill.

> *—maybe deep down, i knew i could do this by*
> *myself. maybe, i just wanted to do it with you.*

i poured my heart into my creativity
to find the solace i couldn't find in you
and look where it's gotten me.

—*without you or the pain you gave me,*
this book wouldn't be possible. thank you.

the dictionary tells me that home is a physical place. so how have i made a person my home? am i defying the social constructs of what a home should be and what it shouldn't be? if it is just a social construct, then does that mean home is a concept we have made up in order to feel more secure with our geographic location despite the fact that you could be at home with the people around you regardless of where you are? or is the physicality of home the most important part of defining home? does it connect your soul to your physical body in a physical place to ensure that you believe this is all real? is home nonexistent when your home is someone else?

how have i made a person my home? i've lived in three different homes but i didn't feel safe in any of those. i felt safe with him. i've lived in three different cities but i didn't feel comfortable in any of those. i did with him. can you live inside someone? or maybe cozy up inside the crevices of his head? or maybe attach yourself like a parasite and dig your roots so deeply within his mind that it fucks with him? break into his skull and his soul and his thoughts down and dig deeper, *dig dig dig*. dig until there is no home left.

does home become nonexistent when you make him your home? or does it become nonexistent when he leaves you? is it nonexistent when he tells you how you broke him when you made him your home? he said: "i was about to combust with the pressure you put on me."

here's an excerpt of a hypothetical conversation that most likely would have happened with him if he hadn't taken my home away from me:

me: "i just piled brick on brick with cement between the cracks to make sure it doesn't break down easily. all this work, all this effort. all the sweet things to whisper in your ear to make our home warm and nice. how can you leave when we just got settled into it?"

him: "our home? my mind is my home. not yours. go back to yours."

me: "i'm afraid to go to my mind alone. i just want to stay with you and your mind and our home."

him: "'*our*' home is about to break because it was meant for one. for me. you cannot live inside another person and expect that to constitute as your home with no repercussions. a home for one can only take so much of two. leave my home alone. leave me alone."

he's gone now with my home in tow. our home at one point, not my home anymore now. is home nonexistent when it has disappeared from your life? or are you just really really far from anything familiar that you've ever known? i wander cluelessly into a stretch of darkness. i wander searching for a home i can stay in. feel safe in, feel comfortable. i wander alone.

do you have multiple homes in multiple people in multiple places? or once you lose a home, are you left to never have a home again? do we only get one home? if we fuck up, we lose it. we lose safety, comfort. we lose our one chance to have it all. or once you've lost a home, can you find another one? second and third chances are much more welcoming than the first. when one front door closes, does another open?

is home nonexistent or is it a social construct to make me feel secure about being with a man who was never good enough for me in the first place? as i bend down on my knees, i watch as the dust and the ash and the debris disintegrate from what was once a home but now a nonexistent pile of *i'm alone and i'm okay*. does it exist if i grab the dust and the ash and the debris and attempt to piece it back together by myself?

— if my home is nonexistent, where am i?

life still seems lonely without you.
i've got nothing to say to you
but i think about you often.
i think about us often.
can you hear my thoughts so loud
they revive the ones you'd forgotten?

i feel angry but i could never be angry with you.
how am i supposed to release it like that?
how am i supposed to let you know it hurt a little?
it hurt, it stung. it burned.

it's a pattern. you fall
right at the end of it.
you're the third to disappear with no explanation.
i let it go because there's nothing else to do.
i drip with so much love,
i can't help but give you more when you ask for less.
you're the fourth to lie to me
with that dirty mouth of yours.

i want to kiss it. i miss it.

i'm better.
tonight i'm not.

the emotions come in waves,
but you dove too deep and never
resurfaced at the horizon.

don't you need to come up to breathe?
how do you live like that? how can you live like that?
i wish you could've taught me before you left.

you said you would, but you never did.

i can only watch from here,
toes curled in the sand and hand up
to shield my eyes from the sun.
it burns so bright.

my eyes burn but i can't tell
if it's the sun or the tears.
my skin burns from the sand sliding
into the wounds you carved
right before you waded in.

i watch your head come up for air finally,
but you can't see me— i'm too far.
i'm way too far.

i open my mouth to scream. maybe
you'll hear me.

but i've got nothing to say to you. i remember,
i remember, i remember.

the sand at my feet has eroded away
and i'm starting to get cold. i guess it's
time to head home.

i'll just think of you often, wondering
if one day you'll ever swim back to me.

> —*stream of conscious:*
> *9PM on 1/28/19*

sometimes victims of pain
aren't always good,
sometimes experiencing that pain
lets them know just what to do
to really hurt someone else

so be careful, young girl
watch out for the signs of hurt
from a man who expects
you to take care of him, to heal him
instead of loving him with purity
like you should
like i've watched many
suffer through

the mistreatment of women
growing thick like vines
too thick to cut down
unless you bring a knife
with you to change
the course of its growth

—a letter to my younger self

lately, i've been yearning for something.
in the in between is a weird place to be.
when your legs are stuck halfway in the quicksand,
and you're slowly sinking down,
the only thing you can think about is
how much deeper you can go
before you disappear at the bottom.
i feel an anxiety building inside of me
as i try and get out.
so i rush.

i always seem to be in a rush.
though, i never really know where i'm going.
it's like time is running out to get to the finish line
of a race i have just began to run.
so, i run as fast as i can.
if i rush, i'll get to the place i'm supposed to end up at.
but the Universe keeps telling me if i do that,
i'll end up to the left
when my destination is on the right.

She repeatedly gives me the same lesson
and i fail to learn it every time.
this time, i hope it will be different.
lately i've been yearning for something.
but it will only come if i learn how to be patient.

i hope i don't sink to the bottom
before i can get out.
i hope i walk slow but just fast enough
to make it to the finish line.
all i can do now is wait and see.
so i wait.

—love is patient, so be patient

me: "what do you know about love, huh?"
him: "not much, only that i love love"
me: "we definitely have that in common then"
him: "oh really now?"

i wonder how we both love love.

i wonder how we both know love is so complicated
but so easy at the same time.

i wonder why we aren't together
but love each other so much.

i wonder why we can't love love together.

me: "probably even more than you"

i wonder if he knows how much i love him.

him: "i'm not sure about that"

does he love me that much too?

i wonder if he thinks about love and thinks of me
i wonder if he knows when i think of love,
i think of him.
i wonder and i wonder and i wonder.

i want to tell him the only reason i love love
is because of him.

but i don't.
i don't reply.

   —a conversation through text: "i love love."

rebuilding from the ground up
takes a bit of time.

i watch the clock as it goes by. i sink
into the sadness and anger

until i've felt so much of it
i cannot anymore.

there— there is where it starts.

i ache and it echoes
reverbrating into my bones. rebuilding
from the ground up means
clearing out the old.

you are allowed to have good memories
with people who are bad for you. you are
allowed to keep them with you
as you start over.

                              —*out with the old,
                              in with the new*

varsha iyer.
for business inquiries: iyervarsha1@gmail.com
@varshnarsh on all social media.